I CAN DO THAT!
Creative play for can-do kids

STICKER SUPERSTAR

T0004994

How to Use This Book

Most of the activities in this book are easy enough for your child to complete without help, but you should provide instructions. Each challenge includes extra stickers that your child can place anywhere they wish.

Build Skills While Playing

Playing with stickers is a marvelous way to hone fine motor skills, hand-eye coordination, and spatial relations. Your child will use stickers to solve mazes, play matching and counting games, and decorate pictures. At the same time, they will:

- practice skills such as decision making and thinking ahead
- enhance the ability to sort and match objects by size, shape, and color
- develop observation skills
- strengthen counting skills
- build confidence
- increase vocabulary
- exercise creativity

Play Together!

Studies show that children learn best when they are engaged with an adult. Stimulate conversation by asking your child to point to and name the animals, objects, colors, or shapes on the page. More important, create meaningful experiences for your child as they learn through play!

SWEET PALS

Put a doughnut sticker on each friend's plate. Then, add a fork and a mug to each table.
Give 3 friends an extra treat!

SLIP AND FALL

Oh no! Rabbit slipped and fell. Help her feel better by adding bandages to her head, arms, and knees. Then, add flowers and butterflies to brighten her day.

COOKIE BASKETS

Fill the baskets with cookies! Be sure each basket contains the same kind of cookies.

MATCH THE UNDERWATER ANIMALS

What animals live in the sea? Put each sticker on its matching shadow.

SAFARI MAZE

Go through the path from ➡ to ➡. What wild animals do you see?
Put the stickers on the matching shadows as you go.

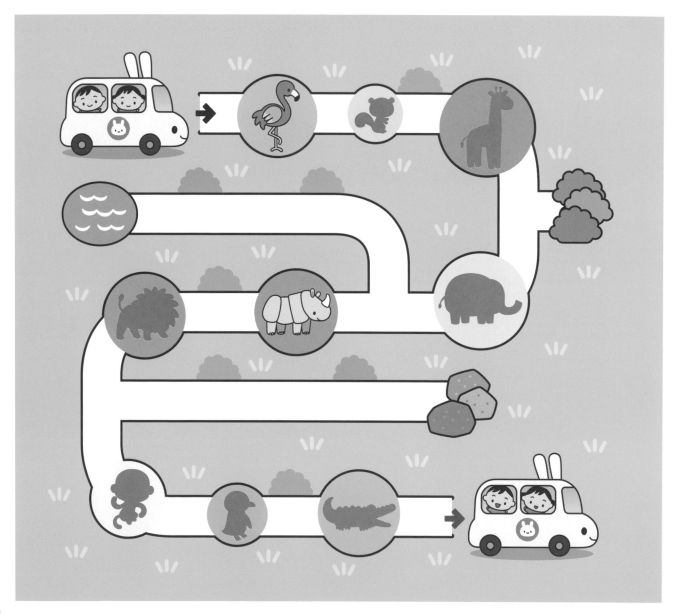

MAKE MATCHING BASKETS

Some fruits are missing! Add fruit stickers to the bottom basket so it matches the top basket.

LET'S MAKE A CAKE!

Decorate this party cake with the candle, fruit, and whipped cream stickers.

MATCH THE SHAPES

Place the stickers on the matching shapes to complete each object.

VEHICLE MATCH

Each box shows the front of a vehicle. Place the sticker that shows the same vehicle from the side on the ▉ .

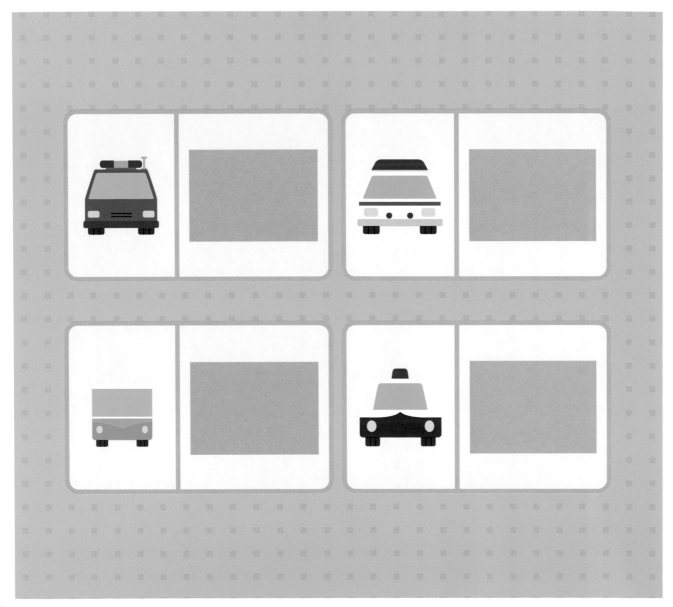

ACORN MAZE

Help the squirrel gather acorns! Follow the path from ➡ to ➡. Always go in the direction of the larger number of acorns. As you pass through each group of acorns, put a squirrel sticker on the space with the larger number.

LET'S GO SHOPPING

Put the stickers on the matching shadows to complete the shopping scene.

LET'S DECORATE A ROOM

Add stickers to decorate the room so the bear friends can have a tea party.

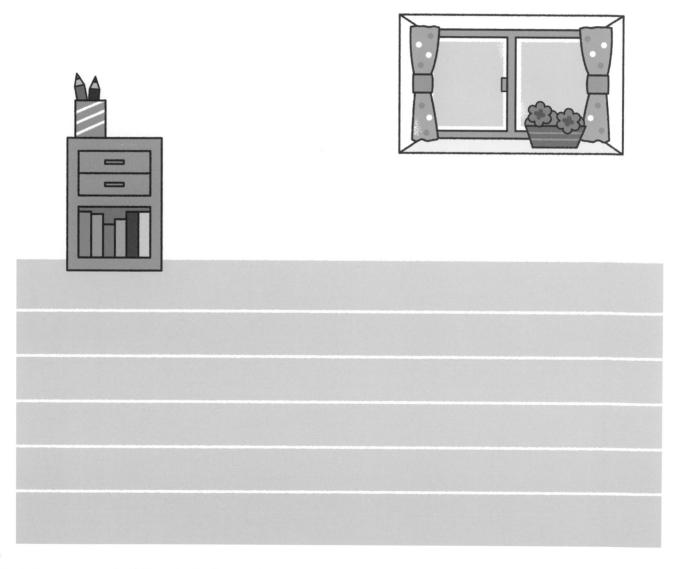

A PIECE OF CAKE

Use stickers to put a piece of cake on each plate. Then, decorate the tables with the flower stickers.

FAMILY DINNER

These animals are dreaming of their favorite meals. Give them dinner by putting matching food stickers on their plates. Add some flowers to the scene, too!

COUNTING 1 AND 2

Count the doughnuts on each plate. Put the matching number sticker in the box next to the plate. Then, add some juice and other treats.

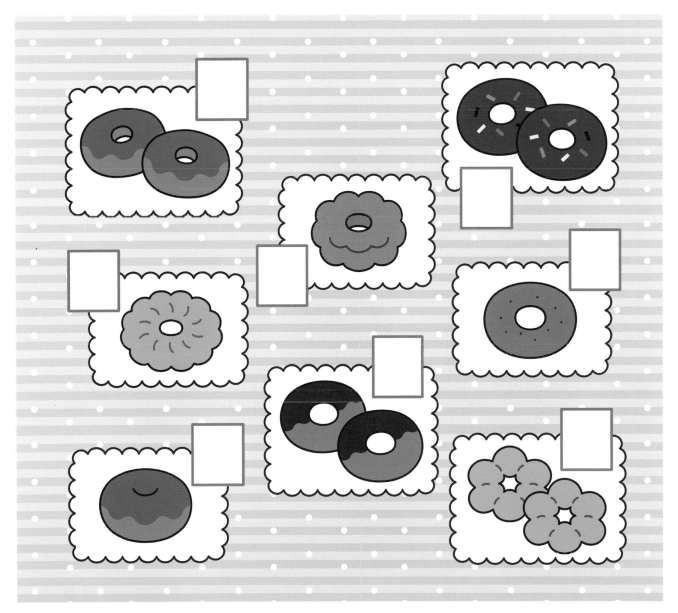

WHICH IS MORE?

Count the objects in each box of the side-by-side pictures. Which box has more? Put a ⭐ on the ⬤ that is in the box with more objects. Add some more fun stickers to the scenes.

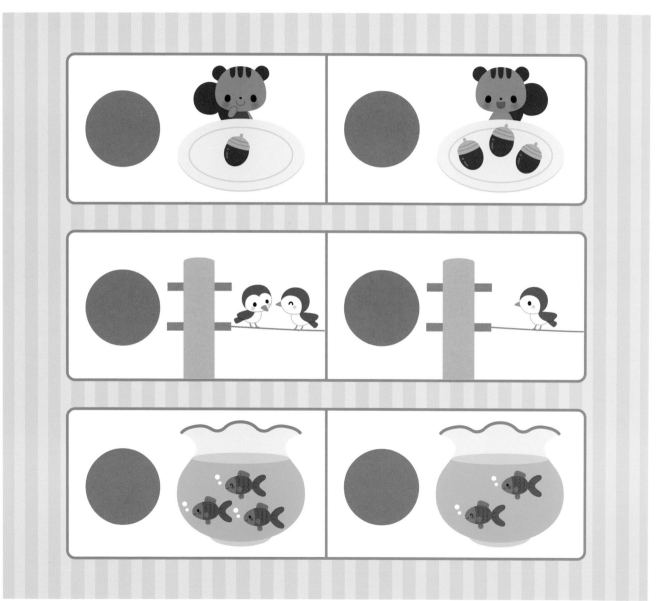

COUNTING CARROTS

Look at how many carrots each zookeeper feeds each rabbit.
Add that number of carrot stickers to each rabbit's dish.

MATCHING BALLOONS

Count the red balloons. Add the same color balloons to the other two baskets so they match the number of red balloons. What other stickers can you add to the sky?

LOADING TRUCKS

Help load trucks! Match the package stickers to their shadows. Then, add a driver next to 2 trucks. Add construction workers and traffic signs to finish the scene!

COUNTING MAZE

Follow the path by putting a 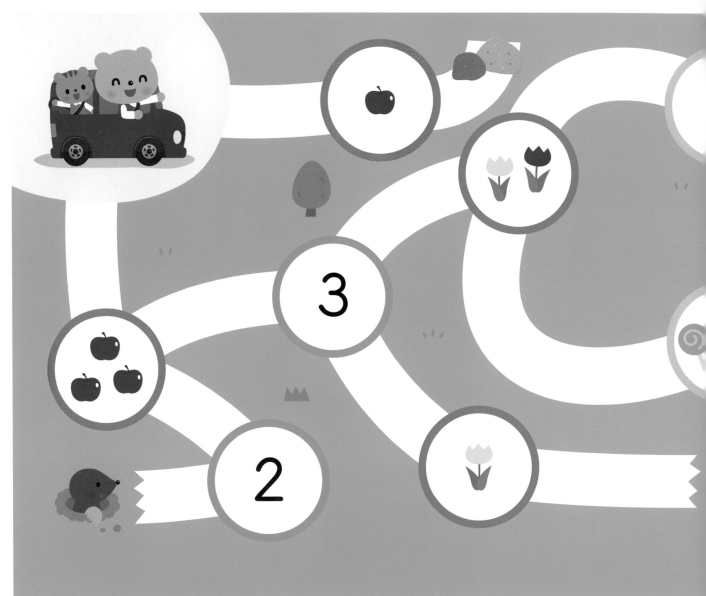 on the circles with more objects or the larger number. Always go in the direction of the larger number. When you're done, add some stickers to the field.

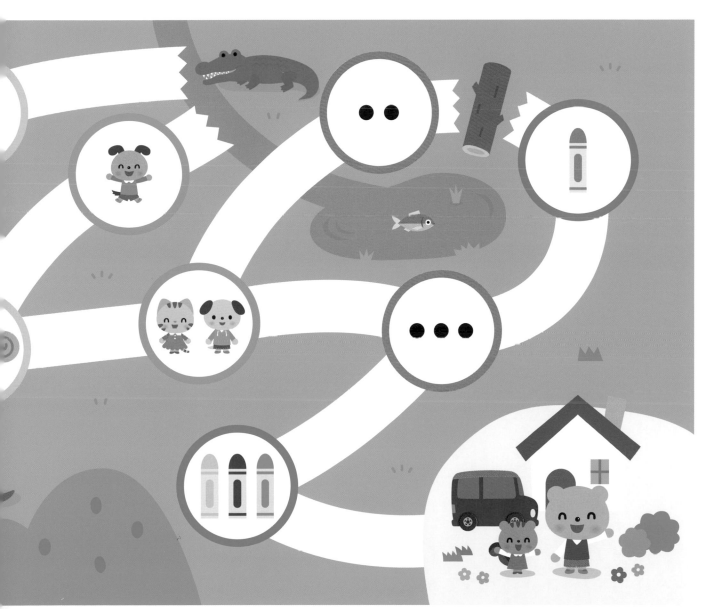

UP IN THE AIR

What do you see in the sky? Add stickers to the blue sky of this picture.

MATCHING FRUIT

Put fruit stickers on the matching shadows to complete the fruit stand.

ANIMAL MATCH

Can you find the hiding animals? Put the stickers on the matching shadows.
Add leaves and flowers to the scene.

AT THE AQUARIUM

Look at the sea animal on each sign. Put the matching sea animal sticker in the tank above it. Add some shell stickers to the tanks, too!

BUSY TOWN

What vehicles do you see in the sky, in the sea, in the city?
Put the stickers on the matching shadows.

BUILDING BLOCKS

Use shape stickers to complete the block castle and towers.
Add more colorful flags and stars!

BEDROOM TIDY-UP

Help keep the bedroom tidy. Put the clothes, shoes, book, and toy stickers in their right places.

MATCHING COLORS

Put yellow fruit stickers on the top plate. Then, put red fruit stickers on the bottom plate.

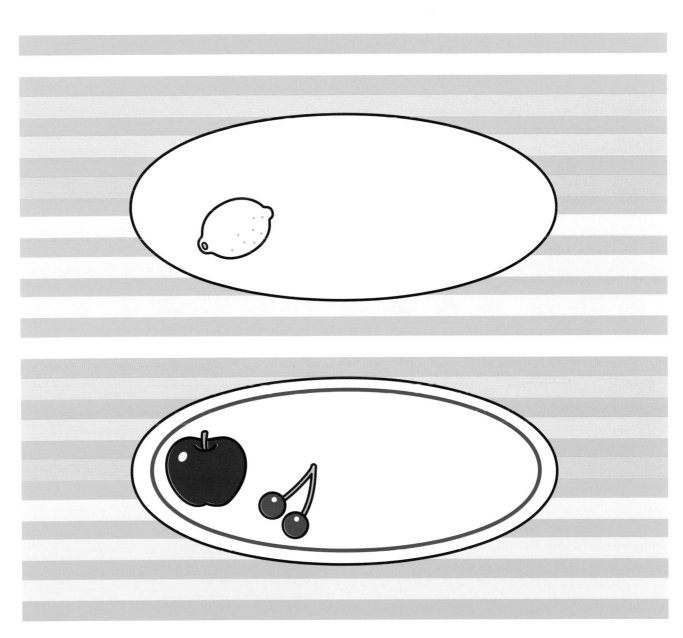

TAKE A RIDE

These animal parents are taking a ride with their children. Put each baby animal sticker next to their parent. Use the extra stickers to decorate the train.

PICTURE MATCH

Let's make matching mountain scenes. Put stickers in the box on the right to fill in the missing images.

TICKTOCK!

Some of the numbers are missing from these clocks. To finish the clocks, put the number stickers in order from 1 to 12. Then, add the hands to each clock. If you need help, look at a clock in your home.

LET'S COUNT TO 10!

Look at these 4 trains. Put the stickers on the matching shadows so each train has 10 parts.

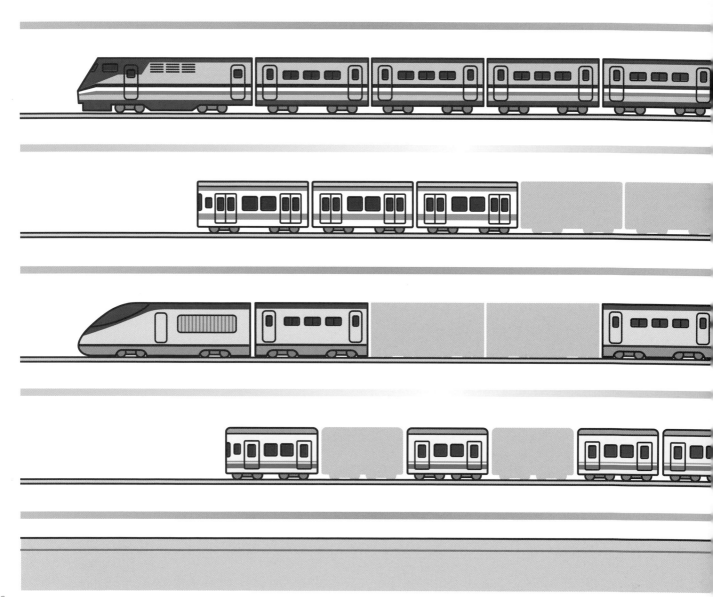

SNACK TIME

Make sure everyone has a delicious snack! Use the stickers to give each child a stack of pancakes. Then, give some children a banana and some children a glass of juice.

TRAIN MAZE

Choo-choo! Go through the maze from ➜ to ➜. As you go, put each train sticker on a shadow.

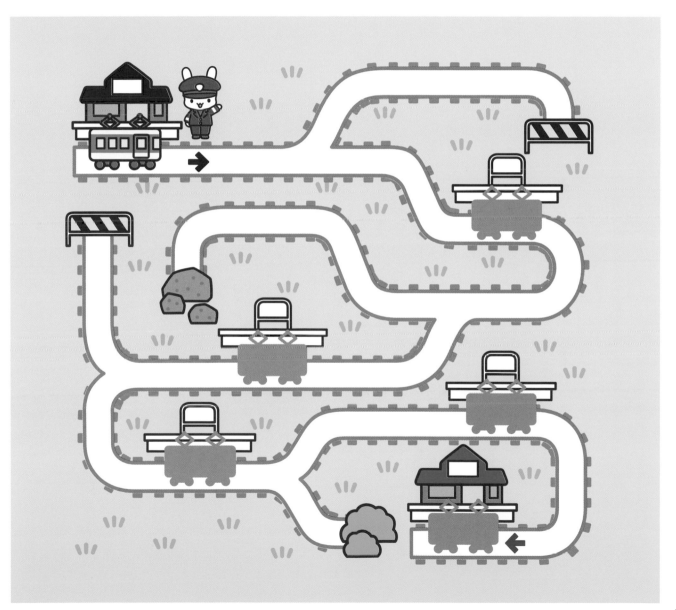

A TRIP TO THE ZOO

Let's visit the animals at the zoo. Place the animal stickers on the matching shadows to complete the busy zoo!

MAIL MAZE

Help the mail carrier deliver the mail! Go through the maze from ➡ to ➡. As you go, place a postcard sticker on each mailbox. Then, add flower and bird stickers to the field.

COMPLETE THE PICTURES

Put the matching sticker next to each vehicle to fill in the picture. Decorate the page with more stickers.

MATCHING GAME

Each box shows an object from above. Beside it, place a sticker that shows the same object from the side. Then, add more fun stickers to the page.

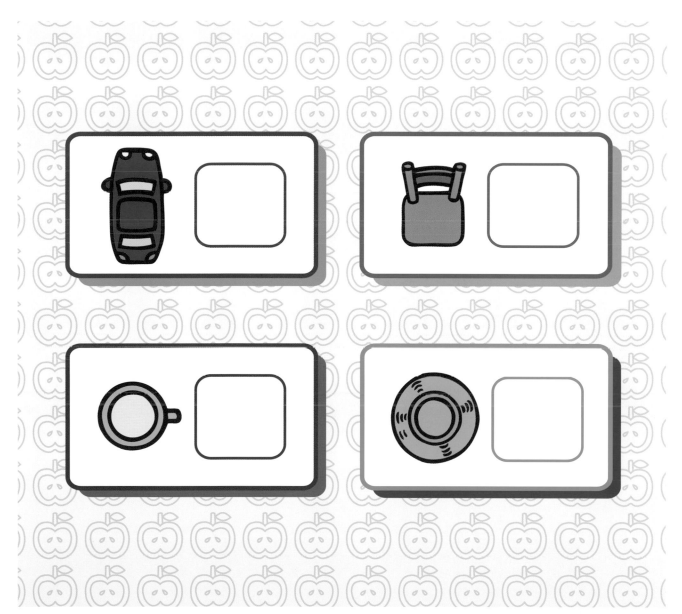

WHAT IS MISSING?

Add candy stickers to the basket on the right so it matches the basket on the left.

WHAT GOES TOGETHER?

Find the stickers that belong in each group, and place them together in the box. Say the name of each group (vehicles, vegetables, animals, and sweet treats) as you go.

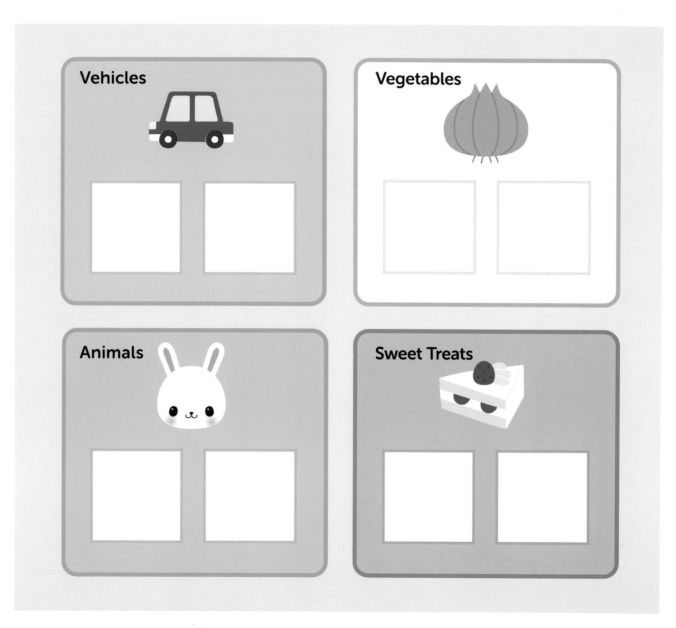

Vehicles

Vegetables

Animals

Sweet Treats